THE ABCS OF DEVELOPMENT

It's About Building Capacity

Linda Swalling Fettig

authorHOUSE®

AuthorHouse™
1663 Liberty Drive, Suite 200
Bloomington, IN 47403
www.authorhouse.com
Phone: 1-800-839-8640

First published by AuthorHouse 8/29/2007

ISBN: 978-1-4343-1490-1 (sc)

Library of Congress Control Number: 2007933572

Printed in the United States of America
Bloomington, Indiana

This book is printed on acid-free paper.

With special thanks to:

My friend, Carla, for encouraging me to write this book,

my Dad for inspiring me to keep learning,

and

my wonderful husband for always believing in me.

The Things That Haven't Been Done Before

Author Unknown

The things that haven't been done before,
those are the things to try.
Columbus dreamed of an unknown shore,
at the rim of the far-flung sky.
And his heart was bold and his faith was strong
as he ventured in dangers new.
And he paid no heed to the jeering throng,
or the fears of the doubting crew.

The many will follow the beaten track
with guideposts along the way.
They live and have for ages back
with a chart for every day.
Someone has told them it's safe to go
on the road he has traveled o'er.
And all that they ever strive to know
are the things that were known before.

The things that haven't been done before
are the tasks worthwhile today.
Are you one of the flock that follows, or
are you one to lead the way?
Are you one of the timid souls that quail
at the jeers of the doubting crew,
Or dare you, whether you win or fail,
strike out for the goal that's new?

Foreword

Many are familiar with the Chinese proverb "*Give a man a fish and you feed him for today. Teach a man to fish and you feed him for a lifetime.*"

There are several messages hidden within this simple saying. The first is the idea of having a *fish given to you*, your organization, or your community for some reason. The fish represents the concept of "entitlement" - you receive the fish because you meet criteria that society has set as deserving of help. Taking this idea to the next level, *teaching you to fish* suggests skill building and planning for the future, which truly sounds like the ideal. My concern is that this proverb assumes that the individual, organization, or community already know how to chew and swallow the fish – in other words, possess the *capacity* to use the resource.

There are countless stories about communities and organizations that were given a fish (resource) for a specific project and even taught how to fish (secure and develop resources), but didn't have the capacity to use the fish. This book is designed to help communities and organizations learn how to "chew and swallow" any fish they are lucky enough to find on their line.

Table of Contents

Tried and True - Case Studies

THE ABC'S OF DEVELOPMENT:

IT'S

ABOUT

BUILDING

CAPACITY

INTRODUCTION:

Just what is this elusive concept called "development"? Is there a difference between community development, economic development, industrial development, and social development? For some practitioners, community development is a focus on the quality of life issues, such as housing, medicine, community facilities, etc., while economic development focuses on job or wealth creation. But development is not that simple, that cut and dried, and definitely not that black and white.

In spite of the many definitions, there are a variety of reasons to think about and pursue development including:

- increasing access to opportunities for local citizens;
- preventing or minimizing chaos by pre-planning;
- ensuring ongoing activity and support for community programs;

- planning for current and future infrastructure needs; and
- enriching the quality of life for residents.

Does it really matter what we call it as long as we reach the desired results? And what are the desired results? Another good question is "Why do we even care about development?" Why not just let nature take its course without any effort on our part? Can individuals or small groups of concerned citizens influence development? These questions and others have led me to write this book and share some of the insights I have gained from more than 25 years of community and economic development experience and my personal passion for capacity issues and developmental challenges.

Back to the earlier question about community and economic development, here are some working definitions. Community development strategies usually include leadership development, housing, child care, community facilities and other projects that improve quality of life for local citizens. Economic development strategies are usually concerned with job or wealth creation including business recruitment, existing business transfer, entrepreneurship assistance, business retention and expansion, and other issues related to the high-tech and low-tech sectors. Development strategies may vary but ALL development, no matter what title we give it, requires capacity. In their book, *Community Development in Perspective* (1989), James Christenson and Jerry Robinson, Jr. state:

> *Development when treated as a normative concept is synonymous with improvement. In this context, development means social transformation in the*

direction of more egalitarian distribution of social goods such as education, health services, housing, participation in political decision making, and other dimensions of people's life chances. It is improvement from the perspective of those to be affected by the change. (p. 9)

Those fancy words mean that development is another way of describing change. It is very important to understand, though, that even wet babies do not always welcome change. Change implies there is something wrong with the way we are doing things now. While the outcome of change or development may be positive, the idea of change is not always welcome and the change process may not always be smooth. John Kotter (1999), writes the following in his book, "*On What Leaders Really Do*":

Of course, all people who are affected by change experience some emotional turmoil. Even changes that appear to be "positive" or "rational" involve loss and uncertainty....be aware of the four most common reasons people resist change. These include: a desire not to lose something of value, a misunderstanding of the change and its implications, a belief that the change does not make sense for the organization, and a low tolerance for change. (p. 31)

There are bookshelves full of volumes that have been written on the topic of change, resistance to change, and both economic and community development. The more books one reads, the more meetings one attends, the more ideas and concepts one tends to collect, the more questions one often has. Understanding development capacity may seem easy but effectively nurturing it definitely is a challenge.

I've come to the conclusion that when all is said and done, development revolves around capacity. In this book, I identify four basic capacities – human, organizational, infrastructure and financial – and allude to a fifth - the capacity to encourage or manage change. Development is really the name for what happens when a change agent introduced into a community or organization results in actions. Building capacity is one way to help communities and organizations deal with change and prepare for their future. It goes back to the adage of giving someone a fish so they can eat today or teaching them to fish so they can eat every day.

The Stanford Research Institute appears to agree with this concept of development and capacity. According to their definition, economic development is "the process by which your community will improve its capacity to grow and develop - economically, educationally, socially, and culturally" (Kotler, as cited in Robert Shively's book, *Economic Development for Small Communities: A Handbook for Economic Development Practitioners and Community Leaders* (2004).

Although the Stanford quote discusses economic development, community and economic development are not two separate concepts. Neither can happen without the other in place. It is like the age-old question, "which comes first, the chicken or the egg?" Development involves both the traditional quality of life issues and economic opportunities. One caution about development - while normally thought of as positive, development can occasionally produce negative results. This is especially true if the development is unplanned, the community is not involved in the planning process, or the change agent is apathy.

Because community cohesiveness and planning are necessary elements for successful development, a community needs to understand the difference between needs and wants, and have a holistic approach to building capacity and planning for development. Building capacity is a way to help prepare communities and organizations to deal with change. A community is constantly changing - it is either:

- declining and struggling to exist,
- growing and struggling to exist,
- growing and struggling to manage growth, or
- growing and thriving.

Status quo simply does not exist in the development arena. Logically, the next question is, how do we build capacity and encourage development? The ideal is to manage and encourage the developmental change, keeping the flow positive. The challenge is to build local capacity to facilitate the management of change – for community or economic development. Capacity also is the key to discovering development opportunities and implementing successful projects. Community and economic development are tightly interwoven. For example, a community needs housing and schools to entice employees while economic growth is required to diversify and expand the tax base to support community needs (such as schools) and infrastructure. Both traditional community development and ongoing economic development are critical to the success of a community.

Although everyone wants to know the secret ingredient or magic trick, there really is no single reason why one community succeeds while another struggles or even fails. The recipe for success requires a dab of inspiration, a generous handful of dedicated volunteers, usually a pinch (or two) of financing, and an occasional smidgen of luck. No matter what label you give development (community or economic), to be successful and maintain long-term capacity it must first be a locally driven grassroots effort. Assistance may come from various entities and resources, but the initial effort, desire for change and willingness to search out assistance and build capacity are locally driven and the results are first felt locally even if there is eventual regional or possible global impact.

How does a community or organization develop the capacity skills it needs? What difference does it make if a community or organization just exists without nurturing capacity? Answering those and other questions is the purpose of this book.

It is important to remember you were not born with your current skill levels, knowledge or abilities - you have accumulated them over time; for some of us it has been over several decades.

Your community or organization will develop capacity the same way, building skills and assets over time. By the same token, time can erode development efforts if capacity is not nurtured and community skills are not shared, mentored and improved.

It also is important to remember that developmental capacity is not a linear process. It is not Step A followed by Step B with guaranteed progress each step of the way. Developmental capacity is not a ladder with a graduation ceremony at the top step. Rather, capacity is a continuous cycle of waxes and wanes, ebbs and flows, inputs and outputs. The inputs and outputs will be discussed further in a later section. Another way to think about capacity is that it defines both the existing and future development abilities of the organization or community. You actually "cap a city" (or limit its development) when you limit the community's ability to build and sustain capacity. To help understand development capacity, let's look at the various capacity sectors.

CAPACITY SECTORS

Webster's Dictionary defines capacity in several ways. It is the "ability to contain, absorb, or receive and hold" and the"quality of being adapted (for something) or susceptible (to something), capability, potentiality and a condition of being qualified or authorized."

However you define it, capacity is the key ingredient for development. While working with a variety of organizations and communities, I have observed four types of capacity needed for development. These are not a continuum, but rather a complex ongoing symbiotic relationship.

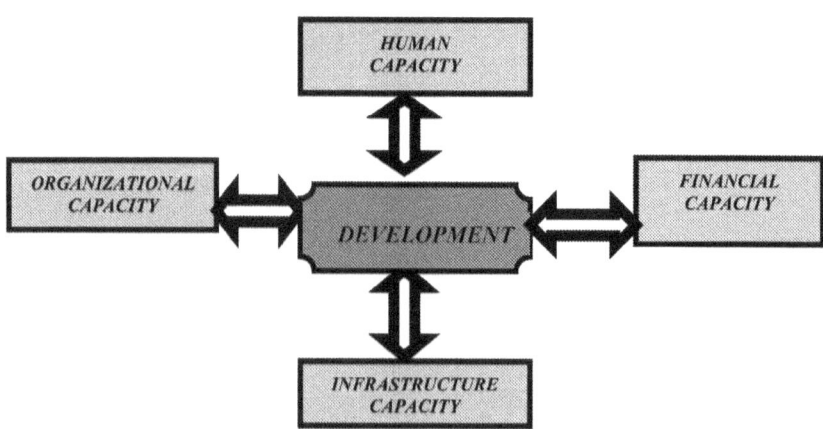

Each part is interrelated to the other capacity categories. In some communities, or even at some stages of development, one capacity may be more active, but all four are required for ongoing development. The book will go into more detail about each capacity category in later chapters, but for now I want to introduce the concepts.

- **HUMAN CAPACITY** is required to understand issues, use resources, learn about opportunities, and bring information to the community. Both leadership and followership are vital to human capacity.

- **ORGANIZATIONAL CAPACITY** is the glue that holds the development puzzle pieces together. We have often heard about synergy where the "whole is greater than the sum of its parts" and this is especially true of organizational capacity. The organization may be formal or informal, as we will see in a later chapter.

- **INFRASTRUCTURE CAPACITY** is essential to meet the current and ever changing needs of businesses and the community while preparing for future development.

- **FINANCIAL CAPACITY** is necessary to influence change, maintain local control of development, and take advantage of opportunities.

So how do the pieces fit together? **HUMAN CAPACITY** recognizes a need and a possible resource then uses either formal or informal **ORGANIZATIONAL CAPACITY** to act as the catalyst for development. **INFRASTRUCTURE** needs are analyzed and appropriate **FINANCIAL** resources and gaps are determined. If a project (housing, infrastructure, jobs, etc.) results from the process, there will be increased opportunity in the community. The success from this project increases the community's developmental capacity and another project might be started or opportunity researched. The cycle results in continuous improvement and an ever growing community capacity for development.

It is like a balloon labeled "capacity". With each input (human, organizational, infrastructure or financial) the capacity balloon expands. The expansion is the physical evidence of the growth in capacity, or the change in a community's capacity. Blowing up a balloon, though, is not done with one quick breath, but rather a number of breaths. Your capacity balloon expands the same way – with a series of breaths (inputs), each time expanding or growing the capacity balloon just a little larger. Unlike real balloons that might burst if overfilled, the capacity balloon has the elastic quality to continuously expand with the proper inputs.

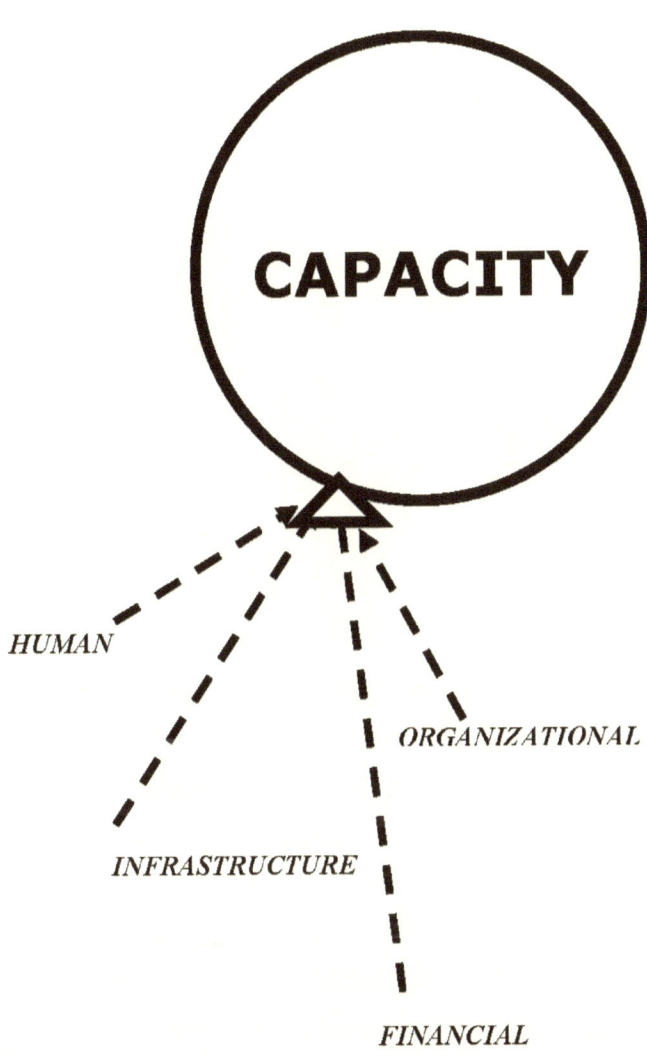

Furthering the balloon analogy, we've all seen balloons that were fully inflated and securely fastened yet began to leak air. If left alone, a balloon eventually will leak enough air to collapse. When we stop adding inputs to our capacity balloon, some capacity eventually leaks out and the balloon begins to contract.

Communities go through cycles where there are significant inputs and the development balloon is full and rising. Then for a variety of reasons, ranging from apathy to lack of additional local capacity, the inputs stop and the development balloon begins to wither. If new capacity inputs are not periodically injected, the capacity balloon will eventually collapse and the community or organization will not have enough capacity to function effectively.

While all capacity elements are critical to long-term success, the crucial factor in a struggling community's revival or further decline is often human capacity. We will examine that in more detail later. First, let's look at why communities exist.

ONCE UPON A TIME

The inscription on the Nebraska State Capitol Building claims, "A community, like an individual, has work to do." But what is that work? To better understand the role communities play in development it is first important to understand why communities, villages, or towns are born.

In his book, *Community Development Theory*, James Cook (n.d.) offers this idea:

A community is a particular type of social system distinguished by the following characteristics:

- *People involved in the system have a sense and recognition of the relationships and common concerns with other members.*
- *The system has longevity, continuity, and is expected to persist.*
- *Its operations depend considerably on voluntary cooperation, with a minimal use (or threat) of sanctions or coercion.*
- *It is multi-functional - the system is expected to produce many things and to be attuned to many dimensions of interactions.*
- *The system is complex, dynamic, and sufficiently large [enough] that instrumental relationships predominate.*

- *Usually there is a geographic element associated with its definition and basic boundaries. (p 9)*

Settlement of the Original Colonies sprung from the basic need of the newly arrived immigrants to have food and shelter. The towns, by necessity, were self-supporting and served as fortresses to protect citizens from known and unknown dangers. As the country's population grew and people moved westward, towns were born to serve congregate needs. Simple mining and logging camps became villages or towns as populations grew and the need for services increased. For farms and ranches, a settlement within reasonable traveling distance (one or two days by horse or buggy) often meant the success or failure of the agricultural endeavor. People needed access to supplies, medical care, and law enforcement.

A trading post or store was usually the first sign of "civilization" as it provided residents with the necessary supplies for life on the frontier. As communities grew and populations expanded to include more women and families, a church and eventually a school were added. For many towns, progress stopped there; others continued to grow adding parks, larger homes, businesses such as law firms, undertakers, newspapers, blacksmiths, buggy and harness repair shops...even jails.

In sections of the country dominated by railroads, towns' locations were based on needs of water and wood to fuel the steam engines. In turn, these towns fostered development of ranches and farms within the comfortable distance of a one or two-day horse or buggy ride. When railroads switched from steam locomotion to other kinds of power, the original founding purpose for many of these small support communities ceased to exist. As automobiles increased the distance a person could travel in a day for supplies, small towns and villages suffered further setbacks as shoppers traveled to larger communities for more selection or additional services.

Understanding a community's history allows us to have pride in previous accomplishments, learn from earlier projects, and develop our sense of place. For thriving communities, it allows us to look at how they adapted to multiple changes in their environment over the course of their existence. For communities that are struggling to survive, it helps us make current decisions based on facts about the community's original purpose. Studying history is important to understanding a community's ability to deal with change and willingness (or unwillingness) to adapt. Many community development efforts are thwarted by a "we've always done it that way" or "we've tried that before and it won't work here" mentality.

Local history is important, but it should not keep us so tied to the past that we cannot move forward. Cook (n.d.) continues his theory on community development by stating: "For a community system to work in terms of return to its members, it must incorporate the *capacity* to continue operations that are satisfactory and to change those that are not effective, (emphasis mine) (p. 23).

In addition to knowing your community history, it also is important to know and understand the history and current basis of your local economy. What was your economy based on historically? Has that changed? What are the implications of your economy for current decisions about development? Are you an industrial-based economy, regional retail economy, service-based economy, information-based economy, agricultural-based economy, or transfer payment-based economy?

Industrial-based economies present certain challenges to any community because the community does not have a voice in the corporate decisions made by industry. An industrial-based economy can be very affluent with many available jobs and a high quality of life, or it can offer a development challenge in terms of lower-paying jobs and need for new and expanded services to meet the growing social needs. A tremendous development challenge arises when a corporate decision closes a facility or reduces the workforce in an industrial-based economy.

Regional retail economies are those communities that have large pull factors (an equation that relates local residents and retail income. For example, a large pull factor indicates people are traveling to a community to shop.) Regional retail centers may spring up when dwindling local populations make it economically infeasible for small towns to continue offering certain products and services thereby requiring residents to travel to neighboring communities. They also may be regional retail centers by design (the Mall of America comes to mind). Human nature allows us to mix business and pleasure, and destination shopping is a bona fide tourism and economic development strategy for some communities.

Service-based economies are based on the ability to offer a variety of services. More small towns are becoming service-based economies as previous retail storefronts are filled with insurance agents, attorneys, accountants, and other professional and service businesses. The communities may only support limited retail, but still have enough population to support local or regional services. Even mid-sized cities are developing into service-based economies as manufacturing outsourcing and online shopping change the economic landscape.

Information-based economies include back office operations of regional, national or multi-national credit cards, insurance, and other information transfer companies not dependent on local customers. Information-based economies may offer opportunities for higher paying jobs and employees looking for a better quality of life. The information age is opening up new development opportunities for small and rural communities that have a trained workforce, the technology infrastructure, and quality of life amenities required to support these industries and their employees. Work-from-home options also become a viable development strategy for those communities with the appropriate telecommunications technology and consumer services.

Agricultural-based economies center on traditional ranches and farms and agricultural support businesses, such as machinery and chemicals. While many rural people think they have an agricultural economy, in truth most rural communities offer a rural or agricultural lifestyle but support a transfer payment economy. What does this mean and why should a community care about its economic base? To encourage progress, it is imperative to have accurate and current data so decisions are not based on erroneous assumptions.

If your community truly has an agricultural economy, your decisions will be based on strengthening the agricultural options, including value-added agriculture and agri-tourism. You also may want to diversify your economy to help ease the oft-extreme fluctuations of the agricultural economy. An agricultural economy is place dependent - in other words, the owner or operator of a farm or ranch is physically tied to that specific location.

While some ranchers or farmers receive federal subsidies, those subsidies also are place dependent (tied to a physical location) Additionally, many farm/ranch families are dependent on off-site incomes where either spouse (and sometimes both) hold jobs in nearby towns. This further ties the agricultural economy to nearby communities.

Transfer payment-based economies are built on non-wage income much of which is mobile. Social security benefits, retirements, investment returns, aid to dependent children, and other support program income is not place specific and recipients can relocate without endangering their income. Your community and economic development decisions need to be based on quality of life issues that help retain current residents and encourage new residents.

Knowing your economic base will help your community make decisions about expenditures of resources, future growth plans, support of existing residents, and economic diversification. Once you understand your local economic base, you are ready to begin a strategic planning process. Strategic planning is a daunting concept and those communities that ignore it are left with no sense of direction or progress toward goals.

Remember the saying "Any road will get you there, if you don't care where you are going"? Planning is an integral part of building capacity whether planning a meeting, project, or for a future goal. There are many ways to encourage public participation in community planning. The formal strategic planning process is one way, but other processes include asset mapping and appreciative inquiry. In addition to strategic planning, there is the concept of strategic thinking. In *Choosing the Future* (1998), author Stuart Wells says, *"strategic thinking can be summed up quite simply:*
- *What seems to be happening?*
- *What possibilities do we face?*
- *What are we going to do about it?" (p. viii)*

Keeping these concepts in mind will make the strategic planning process more meaningful no matter which planning tool you use in your community.

Again, check your local library or favorite website for assistance with planning resources. Or, better yet, contact one of your community and regional resource providers. This is one of many times when your networking opportunities and resource database will prove invaluable.

I was fortunate early in my career to work with Professor Don Littrell, a widely recognized community development guru. In his book on community development, Professor Littrell says, "*As avenues of communication are developed that lead to human interaction, people will tend to broaden their interest. The realization that people in the next town, city, or county share common interests greatly enhances the probability that people will be constantly expanding and broadening their community of interest.*"(p. 7-8)

Many times we talk about community like it has borders carved in stone when the truth is that there are many definitions of community. I always liked Professor Littrell's reference to a community of interest rather than just a geographic location. It also segues to the next idea about the definition of community.

HOW DO YOU SPELL COMMUNITY?

How do you define your community? Does your community stop at the city limits? Does it include the nearest airport, hospital, school, church, farm, and agri-business? Is it a town, a county, a region of the state, or even a multi-state region? Just how do you define your geography and how does that influence your economic opportunities?

Cooperation encourages communities to work as a region for a common goal (regardless of who won the last football game) while still retaining their own local flavor and individuality. Yet, even within this context, a region can be changeable and self-defined. You may work with one set of development partners and communities for one project and a new and different set for the next. This type of regionalism recognizes the "win-win" of partnering. It even has a catchy name "co-opetition" which combines cooperation and competition into one concept.

This functional regionalism has many benefits, especially in community and economic development because it maximizes the resources of local economic development organizations and regional infrastructure. Granting agencies and entities often receive more "bang for the buck" when funding regional projects since more constituents benefit, or a larger constituency may participate. Some funders are even more inclined to invest in regional projects, and sometimes it takes a regional coalition just to accumulate the population base required for certain programs.

The challenge for all of us as we move forward in this very competitive global environment is to network and partner as much as possible, whenever possible. Part of becoming successful depends on our ability to seek out and encourage networking with all it implies - "co-opetition". So, once again, "How do you spell 'community'?"

MONKEY WRENCHES AND OTHER TOOLS

In the world of capacity building, what (or who) are the "monkey wrenches"? There are several types and you may even recognize some of your community volunteers in these groups. Often monkey wrenches are people who get involved, volunteer, and support the community or economic development concept, but who struggle with specific projects.

First is the "*We've always done it this way so why do we need to change?*" group. Following is a story that illustrates the fallacy of this type of thinking.

A young bride was fixing dinner. Her husband observed her cut about 3-4 inches off one end of the roast. He asked why she did that and she wasn't sure. Her Mom always cooked them that way and she would have to ask her. Later she called her Mom and posed the question. Mom said Grandma had taught her to cook them that way and she would need to ask her. So, Mom called Grandma and asked the reason for cutting off the end of the roast. Grandma laughed as she replied, "I had to cut off part of the roast because that was the biggest pan I had."

Many times our communities are still preparing to cook in the smaller pan even though they have purchased new sets of cookware with larger pans. Often the original reason for a specific task or method has been lost, but the tradition has been continued. Identifying the original reason may be difficult and we need to remember if we ask people to change, we are implying they are doing something sub-standard or wrong (why else would you change?). The challenge becomes how to initiate the change with a minimal amount of resistance.

Resistance to change is another topic that has volumes already written containing scores of ideas on how to initiate change and lessen resistance. Again, it is natural for people to resist change. While such resistance can be a challenge to development, it also can be healthy when it keeps us from blindly running from one fad to another.

Next is the "*We've tried that before and it didn't work*" group. What is important for this group to realize is that we are talking about building capacity. Just because something didn't work in the past, doesn't mean that it will never work for an organization or community. A baby falls down many times before it learns to walk, but eventually it walks, runs, hops, skips, and jumps. Of course, this doesn't imply that you continually set yourself up to fail or fall. Building capacity will help you learn to walk and maybe eventually run with your projects. Your community or organization needs to analyze current capacity, resources, and needs when determining what projects to pursue.

Last, but not least, are the coffee shop "*con*" artists. You know these people; they take the "con" side of every argument. Like Grumpy in the Snow White movie, they don't know what it is but they know "they're a'gin it". "Con" artists are closely related to *CAVE* people (Citizens Against Virtually

Everything) and to those who believe in the *BANANA* theory of development (Build Absolutely Nothing Anywhere Near Anyone). It may take a real effort to draw these folks into a project, but it can be done.

One community challenged the naysayers to go an entire day without grumping or saying anything negative about the community. What happened in this town could also happen in yours. The con artists had not realized how their negative input was affecting proposed projects. The community acknowledged the need to have someone honestly questioning projects and plans. Both sides gave a little and the community replaced some of the negative atmosphere with a sounding board for ideas.

While monkey wrenches might be considered negative tools, there are other positive tools. Networking and resource education can be invaluable to a community for technical assistance and possibly financial assistance. Not every community will have access to the same resources, but most will have access to at least some listed here:

- Utilities including gas, electricity, and communications. Most utilities offer some degree of technical assistance and many offer specific development programs and mentoring. Growing a business or community naturally helps increase the potential customer base and makes the growth of their utility business a more promising prospect.

- Extension educators from land grant universities offer a wealth of technical assistance and literature.

Some may offer hands-on program assistance. Each state's extension program offers a unique set of services so build capacity by learning what assistance is available in your area.

- Local development groups, such as Chambers of Commerce or Community Clubs, economic development organizations that are funded with public dollars or a combination of public and private dollars, and private development organizations which are supported by memberships or local contributions are great resources for technical assistance and possibly identifying funding opportunities.

- Regional community and economic development organizations offer another level of technical assistance. More organizations are being formed to maximize the scarce local resources and to take advantage of larger volunteer pools. The regional development organizations may be local grassroots efforts combined for specific projects, such as housing, or formal regional organizations developed for community and economic development. There also are state and federal regional organizations, such as Resource Conservation and Development Districts, Councils of Governments, or Economic Development Administration Development Districts.

- Although state agencies may go by slightly different names from one state to another, usually there is a state Department of Commerce or Department of Economic Development. Other helpful state agencies include the departments of Agriculture, Environmental Quality, Health and Human Services, and Labor. Tourism may be included in the Department of Commerce or Economic Development. In some states, Tourism is a stand-alone agency. All of these agencies generally offer various types of technical assistance and funding for specific projects.

Another tool to consider is community or organizational alumni. Alumni can offer their expertise, skills and knowledge on specific projects. They can be an excellent source for donations to a project or a community foundation. They may also consider expanding or starting a business in your community. Be sure you include all alumni in your development tool kit. Many communities regularly inform alumni of community needs, special events, and opportunities in which they can participate via newsletters and other mailings. With the advent of the Internet, many communities also target their alumni with special pages on the town website. However you choose to interact with them, be sure that alumni communications is a key part of your overall capacity development strategy.

Now, let's take a closer look at each of the four capacity components starting with the **HUMAN CAPACITY**.

HUMAN CAPACITY

VOLUNTEERS ARE PRICELESS

Several years ago I was involved with "Community Builders", a grassroots capacity building program. One evening while preparing for a session, I noticed something about the word community. The first part of the word is *commun(e)* which Webster defines as "to talk intimately or to be in close rapport". The last part of the word is *unity* which Webster defines as "a quality of being one in spirit, sentiment, or purpose". The very center of the word is the letter "u". "U" (you) are what makes community.

"U", the volunteers are literally priceless. For most communities, budget constraints do not allow the level of service needed for many projects, but volunteers give freely of their time and talents, enriching the communities and helping to build the human capacity needed for development. Community betterment programs often track volunteer hours and report a dollar figure donated to the community. The community is usually amazed at the value of donated time and energy.

In addition to being priceless, volunteers have unknowingly contributed to a new math concept that I call the "***Power of One***". While many projects involve groups to accomplish a final goal, the original idea usually is generated by one or two people who have taken time to research a need, attend a seminar, visit a neighboring community, or surf the net trying to find answers for local problems. Noted anthropologist Margaret Mead said, "Never believe that a few caring people can't change the world. For, indeed that's all who ever have".

In some cases an entire project can be completed by one dedicated volunteer who writes the grant application, attends the seminar, paints the room, and stuffs the envelopes, etc. Some projects, however, take a concerted volunteer effort and possibly even paid resources. Another math concept derived from human capacity is "synergy" where the power or energy of the whole is greater than the sum of its parts. We see this demonstrated repeatedly when volunteers band together to accomplish a monumental task.

The "***Power of One***" coupled with the "**synergy**" of a committed group can be the catalyst for tremendous community growth and capacity building. While all the capacity components are necessary for varying degrees of success, human capacity is the linchpin. So how does a community or organization foster the volunteer development that is so critical?

Volunteer development is a major component in all community and economic development efforts. Traditionally, volunteers have performed certain community functions thereby freeing community officials to concentrate financial resources on other needs. While volunteer activities vary from community to community, there is no doubt about their impact on community development and about the growing volunteer void experienced by most communities.

In the forward for Robert Shively's book, *Economic Development for Small Communities: A Handbook for Economic Development Practitioners and Community Leaders* (2004), David Kolzow, notes:

> *The traditional sources of leadership - such as local banks, home-grown businesses, civic organizations, etc. - are disappearing in the wake of mergers and acquisitions, branch plants, transient managers, and "brain drains". Clearly, the development of new leaders is critical, but it is even more critical that these individuals possess the kind of collaborative skills that enable them to work together productively to solve increasingly complex local social and economic community problems. (pg vii)*

In addition to the situations mentioned above, the advent of the two-income family limits the amount of time individuals have to spend at home and, thereby, limits the time they have to donate to the community or causes they support. To help reverse the volunteer shortage trend, we may need to rethink our concept of the volunteer as the person who has "nothing else to do". If we recognize that potential volunteers are very busy individuals with many choices for their time, it will be easier to understand, and subsequently nurture a volunteer base.

One way to keep fresh ideas and faces in the volunteer base is to play the "name game" at committee meetings to generate potential new volunteers. The name game is a simple matrix designed to fit your own community. On the horizontal side, list geographic areas of the community (north of the school, south of the creek, east of the courthouse, etc.). Use whatever is meaningful in your community and don't forget to include geographic categories for people who do not live within the city limits. There is no magic to the number of columns created and if you post this on the wall on large sheets, you can make multiple columns. On the vertical side, list categories of individuals (youth, farmer, rancher, professional, retiree, teacher, factory worker, service provider, golfer, etc.) Again, there is no required number of categories. Get creative, as these categories will help you think of new people to invite.

Here is a sample:

	North of school	South of the creek	East of the courthouse	West of the highway	Out of town
Youth					
Farmer					
Retiree					
Teacher					

Next, hang the matrix on the wall and start filling in names where the squares intersect on the matrix. Make squares large enough to list several names in each category. You will be surprised how one name spoken out loud or written on the chart seems to generate another suggestion. The final step is to then personally invite those identified by the "name game" to be a part of your project. Even if you only gain two or three new members this way, you have increased your volunteer base and strengthened your project.

Another way to enlarge your volunteer base is to keep a database of specific skills. Everyone in a community has something to contribute – encourage your committees to ask people three things they would be willing to do to help a project. These can be as simple as babysitting so others can attend a meeting, baking cookies for the meeting or the fundraiser, making phone calls, helping at information booths, or sealing and stamping envelopes. Of course, it also is nice to be able to identify specific skills, such as knowing how to use a chain saw, operate a computer program, or possessing good construction skills, etc. Once these various skills are identified, enter them into a computer database and keep it current. Then when a specific task is required, you will have a starting place to request assistance and to best use your human capacity.

A word of caution, however, about operating databases, while volunteers may indicate they can bake cookies, they did not mean every Saturday for the rest of their lives. Volunteers often suffer burn out from their willingness to help and people too often taking advantage of that willingness. With time being such a precious commodity, people are more apt to respond favorably to very specific requests. For example, you don't need cookies; you need three-dozen cookies on May 2. That is a commitment the volunteer can more easily relate to, complete, and it is a win-win for all involved. You get the help and the volunteer can feel part of the project without making an eternal commitment.

While volunteers need recognition, not all volunteers want to be recognized in the same way. Some people appreciate a simple spoken "thank you" while others crave the occasional spotlight. Recognition might include listing your volunteers' names in the program for your annual dinner. Group photos of volunteers taken at various projects are a good way to show community support. Small items with your organization's logo may help spread your message while making volunteers feel appreciated. Budgets will ultimately dictate what can be done, but a simple "thank you" can always be spoken or shared. When developing your human capacity look for ways to network with other communities and design recognition options to meet the needs of volunteers.

Many states have formal community betterment programs such as Nebraska's Community Improvement Program (NCIP), Missouri's Community Betterment (MCB), Kansas Pride, and similar programs in Oklahoma, Arkansas, and other states. If your community is not participating in such a program, contact your resource providers to learn what is available in your area.

WHICH WAY DID THE PARADE GO?

Well-organized parades follow a planned route and a happy and proud leader shows the way. That arrangement may be great for parades, but leadership in general can be uncomfortable for some people, especially volunteer leadership that needs to rely on the goodwill of followers. Leadership in community and economic development is often compared to herding cats. Each cat has its own idea about where to go and how to get there. Likewise community volunteers often have agendas and preferred paths of progress. So where do leaders come from and where do they acquire the needed skills?

It is important to note that leadership is a vital requirement of human capacity, but does not necessarily require a battalion of leaders. In fact, if you initially have a battalion of leaders, you probably don't have enough volunteers to complete any projects. John Kotter, *On What Leaders Really Do* (1999) offers: "*Major renewal programs often start with just one or two people. In cases of successful transformation efforts, the leadership coalition grows and grows over time.*" (p. 79)

Offering opportunities for those interested in leadership to learn skills is vital to a vibrant ongoing development program. In the *Leadership Secrets of Attila the Hun (1987),* Wess Roberts suggests,

Any extraordinary method for accelerating the acquisition of leadership skills, attitudes and attributes is yet to be discovered. For the time being, as in centuries past, it seems to be the nature of the human being to acquire leadership traits a little at a time - building upon previously learned precepts. (p xvii)

Roberts further states: *"Leadership is the privilege to have the responsibility to direct the actions of others in carrying out the purposes of the organization, at varying levels of authority and with accountability for both successful and failed endeavors." (p. xiv).*

What an interesting concept – accountability for both successes and failures! While I agree with the comment, I can hear the whir of other people's thoughts, "If I am the leader I get to claim the victories, but I also have to acknowledge the failures? Okay, count me out. I have enough headaches with my job and family. I don't need the extra stress and I don't even know how to be a leader." Of course, they are right about the added stress, but building leadership capacity is critical to any community's ongoing development. Finding opportunities for volunteers to assume responsibility will eventually enrich your community or organizational human capacity.

The one leadership topic not as readily written about is what I call "followership". Every project needs worker bees as well as the queen bee. Roberts continues his leadership comments... *"Without subordinates there can be no leaders. Leaders are, therefore, caretakers of the interests and well-being of those and the purposes they serve." (p 22)*

This comment on subordinates or volunteers may be the focal point of human capacity development. With no followers, there is no need for a leader. Followership is the strength required to go from concept to concrete project. Followers are most often the unsung heroes and heroines who build our future human capacity and help develop our community or organizational potential. In his book, *Leading Change, the Argument for Values-Based Leadership"*, James O'Toole (1996) suggests: "*Since the 1980s, it has become more widely accepted that change is the prime task of leaders and that the best measure of effective leadership is the behavior of followers. To the extent the followers embrace needed change, leaders can be said to be effective."(p. 158)*

Building human capacity needs to focus on building the capacity within subordinates or volunteers, as well as leaders. This may include everything from volunteers eventually assuming leadership roles to choosing never to assume the leading role, but supporting those who become leaders. Building human capacity may involve a formal leadership program or graduated leadership opportunity. It may take the form of encouraging specific skills development in followers. There is no absolute right way to build human capacity and no single path that is the best for every volunteer, community or organization to follow.

A basic understanding of leadership and followership, and their associated skills, challenges, and opportunities is vital for communities or organizations striving to build human capacity. Again, libraries and bookstores are full of volumes dealing with leadership. I just want to emphasize followership is as vital to development as leadership.

SPARK PLUGS

In an engine, fuel vapors are ignited by the spark plug starting the combustion process. Just like an engine needs a spark plug, so, too, communities sometimes need a human spark plug to energize and motivate the volunteers, and encourage the use of existing resources. The children's story of the "Little Engine that Could" illustrates how a spark plug attitude and positive energy helps us work toward goals. I'm sure you have heard the saying "Whether you think you can, or you think you can't, you are right". So why not think positively?

We have all seen communities spring back to life after many years being dormant. They seem to get recharged overnight and begin to reinvest in the development process. This phenomenon can often be traced to a "spark plug" - someone in the community who gets excited about possibilities and excites others with their enthusiasm.

Sometimes this spark plug is a person who left and returns home with ideas and projects they have seen working in other communities. Sometimes the spark plug is a person who attended a meeting or seminar and caught development fever. Sometimes they just recognize an unmet need and become determined to find a solution. Whatever their reason, they are often the catalyst for either initiating or reinvigorating development. They add spark to the process.

GRANDMAS AND OTHER CHEERLEADERS

Another invaluable category of human capacity is what I call "Grandmas and Other Cheerleaders". A colleague shared this charming story with me that really brings home the point.

A family moved into a new community and attended church their first Sunday. After Sunday school the parents asked the little boy about his class. He said it was interesting. They asked who his teacher was and he replied, "I don't know her name but I know WHO she is." Curious, the parents asked who she was. The child said, "Jesus' Grandma". The Mom thought this was strange and asked how the boy knew. He answered, "She must be his Grandma, because she spent the whole time talking about him and showing us his picture!"

So who is the grandma or cheerleader for your community? Who carries community brochures (you do have one, right?) in their briefcases or purses? Who shares the brochure with the person on the plane, with resource providers, agencies, and funders? Who is marketing your community?

Grandmas and cheerleaders make great mentors, as their enthusiasm for community projects can be contagious. Encourage them to help someone new to the community or new to volunteering become acquainted with the projects. Some communities have informal mentoring programs where a new volunteer is paired with a project buddy to ease the discomfort of being the new kid on the block.

In many communities it is easy to find naysayers, or another name for them: "con" artists. Just go to the coffee shop and listen to the comments. We can easily rally around local sports events and we should do the same for community efforts. Volunteers are invaluable for the skills they contribute to specific projects. Similarly, grandmas and cheerleaders are invaluable for the enthusiasm they generate for your community and its development.

CELEBRATE THE HUMAN CAPACITY

The Heartland Center for Leadership Development published a list called *Clues to Rural Community Survival.* Vicki Luther and Milan Wall, co-founders of the center, include this comment in that list:

Willingness to Invest in the Future - Some of the brick and mortar investments are most apparent, but these communities also invest in their future in other ways. Residents invest time and energy in community improvement projects and they concern themselves with how what they are doing today will impact on the lives of their children and grandchildren in the future."

As you build capacity in your community or organization, find ways to promote pride in your accomplishments. Plan media events to tell your story, organize a "fam" (familiarization) tour to showcase your efforts for state and regional resource providers, and most of all encourage local citizens to be proud of the accomplishments and progress. In Robert Shively's article, "*Small Town Economic Development: Principles of Organization"* (1997) he offers this thought on the value of leadership:

Weak leadership, an inefficient organizational structure, and inadequate funding (usually a function of weak leadership) are the most frequent causes of failed economic development programs. Economic developers do not have the luxury of selecting community leaders; they inherit them. By expanding the pool from which community leaders are drawn, a community can gradually improve the quality and effectiveness of its leadership and, consequently, its economic development program. (p 46)

This same advice is true for community development and organizational development. Celebrate your human capacity because it is a critical factor in capacity building. Without ongoing development of your community's or organization's human capacity, you will burn out your existing pool of volunteers and the other capacity sectors will become ineffective because no one is coordinating the efforts. Speaking of coordinating efforts, let's look next at **ORGANIZATIONAL CAPACITY.**

ORGANIZATIONAL CAPACITY

WHO ARE YOU?

The first question you need to answer involves your reason for existing as a community or organization. Here's the litmus test:

- What is your "business" (purpose)?
- Who is your "customer"?
- What is the identity or image you wish to project?

These questions are equally applicable to communities or organizations. Communities and organizations must serve a purpose or they will cease to exist.

How does your community answer these basic organizational questions? Next, how does your development organization answer the same questions? Additionally, organizations need to ask what needs they fill in the community.

Is another group already formed to address those needs? Would your efforts be better utilized helping an existing group gain capacity, or is starting a new project or organization the best answer considering the available resources?

Now that you have agreed upon your business, customer, and identity you can get down to the serious work of building organizational capacity to realize your goals. Once again, we are back to planning.

PLANNING TO WORK

Every group has its own acronyms - development or capacity building groups are no exception. Almost all resources are known by the acronym for their agency. Programs often have long and complicated names that can be difficult to remember and acronyms help us communicate better within our fields and professions. In my work, I have created an acronym for the development process and partnering – **AND:**

Analyze the situation,

Network to learn about opportunities and resources,

Develop the project.

Use this simple formula to help write your work plan. Although everyone wants to get right to the project and the ribbon cutting, the initial planning stage is an important way to involve people in sharing ideas for change. The plan can help determine what resources are available and what additional resources are needed. A shared plan can serve as a good public relations tool and build community support for a proposed project or for the development organization itself.

If you first look for projects that have local appeal and commitment, it will be easier to recruit a volunteer base and instill local pride. If your project requires financial assistance, a local match may be required. The match may have to be hard dollars (cash) for some projects and in-kind (donations of time, materials, skills) for other funders. Building local support now for your organization will assist in securing future project funding.

It also is important to build and maintain ongoing organizational support to take advantage of development opportunities that involve shorter turn-around times. In his book *On What Leaders Really Do,* (1999) John Kotter acknowledges the need for readiness, *"In this environment, I now think a twenty-first century, change-ready organization would keep urgency up and complacency down all the time, not just at the beginning of a major change effort. Such an organization would stress teamwork so that it could put together a change-driving coalition on short notice."* *(p.20)*

While a work plan should not be carved in stone in order to take full advantage of unforeseen or changing opportunities, it is helpful if the plan includes a general sense of direction. According to Jack Ruff, one of my co-workers, "Remember that in the movie, *Field of Dreams*, they didn't build a bowling alley and hope for a baseball team."

Plans should be thought of as road maps. Maps mark highways as well as lesser-traveled roads. While the path to a specific goal may not follow the faster metaphoric 'highway", you still arrive at your destination and maybe enjoy the trip more as long as your plan allows you to move forward with those resources available to you.

At some point in a community's or organization's capacity building program, the projects become too large and complex for volunteers to manage without some coordination and staff assistance. In *Changing by Design* (1997), author Douglas Eadie comments: "

> *Organizations are complex and dynamic puzzles consisting of ever-shifting pieces. There are the people organized into entities, such as the board, the management team, departments, divisions, programs, projects, and other units. There are the systems and processes that support the people: strategic and operational planning; budget preparation and management; financial management; information management; and many others." (p.50)*

As Eadie points out, organizational capacity building creates its own set of questions and options. The first organizational capacity building issue is often how do we organize?

THE ORGANIZATIONAL DILEMMA

In his book, *The Theory and Practice of Community Development,* (n.d.) Professor Littrell offers: *"A highly structured community development organization is not a pre-requisite for community development. A group does not need to have officers, by-laws, etc., to be a functioning group." (p.32).* A mission statement may help you verbalize your purpose and determine your organizational needs. The easiest way to write a mission statement is to fill in the blanks on this phrase: **WE** (our organization) do **WHAT** (specific purpose) for **WHOM** (intended constituents).

However, many communities eventually reach a point where a formal organization is needed, sometimes to present a united front, sometimes to acquire funding. The challenge is to analyze your community's needs to determine if, and when a formal organization is needed and what other type of organization or organizations may meet your community's or project needs. Do you need to start a new organization to meet those needs or can you partner with an existing group? Can you function as a volunteer group or do you need more formal structure to receive funding or complete your project?

If you decide you need formal organization, you will need to choose whether it should be a for-profit or not-for-profit. If you select not-for-profit, you will need to understand the a variety of 501c designations, specific Internal Revenue Service rules governing the different types of 501c entities, and what activities each may legally conduct. You should seek qualified legal advice for assistance on selecting the correct formal organizational structure. The following general information from the IRS website (www.irs.gov) is included to facilitate discussions with your legal representative.

501(c) WHAT?

- **501(c)3**-PURPOSE: charitable, religious, educational, scientific, literary, testing for public safety, fostering national or international amateur sports competition, and the prevention of cruelty to children or animals. No part of the net earnings of a 501c3 organization may inure to the benefit of any private shareholder or individual. Further, 501c3 organizations are restricted in the amount of political and legislative (lobbying) they may conduct.

- **501(c)4** - PURPOSE: social welfare organization operating primarily to further the common good and general welfare of the people of the community. There are many considerations about the appropriate lobbying activities of a 501(c)4.

- **501(c)6** - PURPOSE: a business league formed to promote common interests (many chambers of commerce are formed under this guideline). No earnings may benefit any private shareholder or individual. Lobbying is allowed with certain stipulations.

Additionally, there are:

- Fraternal Societies under 501(c)8 and 501(c)10
- Labor and Agricultural Organizations under 501(c)5
- Social Clubs under 501(c)5
- Veterans Organizations under 501(c)9 and 501(c)23

Differentiating between the 501s can be complicated and requires legal advice to ensure your organization is choosing the best classification for short-term and long-term goals. It also is important to know if your entity will seek grant support because not all 501s are equally able to receive grant funds. Some organizations actually form two separate, but cooperating legal entities to allow the work of the organization to be properly classified and supported by an entity that can receive grants. Another option is to partner with a community entity that is an eligible grant recipient to complete projects requiring grant assistance. Again, discuss these and other options with your legal counsel.

Think about what type of organization can best access the resources needed for your community's growth. There is no single organizational structure that fits every community's needs and a single organization probably will not have all the answers. A local or regional partnership may offer a better solution and begin to build capacity on a wider basis. Many communities have active chambers, economic development boards, and tourism groups as well as library boards, school supporters, and other local organizations. Finding a way for existing organizations to cooperate may offer the best solution.

Some communities have multiple development-oriented organizations and various foundations. These communities have successfully encouraged communications among the groups, and established priorities for benevolent gifts. They have learned the secret of maximizing all components of capacity building as they share volunteers, organizational support, financial resources and infrastructure needed to accomplish goals.

Once you are organized, you can begin working on your plan. There is a component of organizational behavior that is critical for all communities to understand. Each organization, whether formal or informal, will go through the phases of "forming, storming, norming, performing, and adjourning" (*Managing Organizations,* Thomas Duening & John Ivancevich, 2003, p. 370-371). It is helpful to recognize which stage of normal development behavior your organization is in when assessing progress and determining the next steps for organizational capacity building.

FORMING AND STORMING

FORMING: In this stage, you are literally coming together (often for the first time), becoming acquainted and beginning to sketch out a mission. You are agreeing to meet and trying to reach an objective. This is when a community often conducts surveys, has focus group meetings, forms task forces and committees, or hosts town hall meetings.

When facilitating during the forming stage, I allow the audience to vote for as many projects as they wish - providing they are willing to be part of that committee and project. Audience members sign their names by the project(s) they support. I then ask for a "contact person" for each committee so I can share appropriate resources. A contact person is not that scary, intimidating word – chair. I have never had a meeting where someone didn't volunteer to be a committee contact and set up the next committee meeting. Viola! The committees are formed and the process encourages public commitment to both the project and the organization. After the "forming" stage, when committees are organized and projects are chosen comes the organizational stage known as "storming".

STORMING: Organization members are now trying to understand the mission and come to consensus about the function, rules, guidelines, etc. Individually, they are assessing their own involvement in the mission and overall success of the group. Some members may choose not to continue during this stage. This parting of the ways does not mean they don't support the organization or project. Rather, it may be a realistic evaluation of their time commitment to participate compared with family scheduling conflicts or other reasons. Members who disengage should be thanked for their efforts to date and asked to continue championing the project. Storming, while often painful, is still part of the normal organizational process.

NORMING: The remaining members become more comfortable with the organizational expectations and each other. They begin to form the true basis of future teamwork. Fine-tuning the organization or proposed project are associated with the norming stage. Funding considerations bridge both the norming and performing stages as the group considers the question of financial capacity. For some organizations, norming is blended right into performing.

PERFORMING: The organization is now actively engaged in projects. This is the visible stage where recommendations are made and accepted, progress is measured, and organizations make an impact.

Performing is a rewarding stage for many members. At this point, an organization may hire staff or continue as a volunteer organization. Even if staff is hired, volunteers are still needed to help with specific projects. The "performing" stage requires an entire orchestra with various instruments (skills), not just a good conductor waving a baton to make the music happen.

An excellent evaluation tool is the Kiva Process and asks three simple questions -

1. What are we doing that we should continue to do?
2. What are we doing that we should stop doing?
3. What are we not doing that we should plan to start doing?

Carefully, evaluate each project and your organizational resources to make the best investment of your capacity. Sometimes a community or organization continues holding an event or sponsoring an activity long after the community no longer finds it valuable or relevant. It is often difficult to permit ourselves to discontinue projects. However, every organization with limited resources needs to weigh existing projects against new ones to make the best use of resources. No group, organization, or even community has all the answers to every problem. Even though there may be a great deal of concern about a specific community topic, it may not be within your capabilities to remedy the situation.

For example, laws may restrict signage along the highway. One option may be to find ways to change the laws. Another option is to choose a different project, one with more local impact. Neither option is wrong; a community needs to evaluate its capacity and decide where to "spend" its development capacity.

If an organization exists over a long period of time, it may, and very well will, recycle through the previously listed stages as goals change and new projects are defined. Recycling through earlier stages does not mean the organization is dysfunctional. Sometimes new projects re-trigger the "storming" stage as the group figures out new roles consistent with group skills and project needs. In fact, every time you change staff or members, the organization needs to revisit the forming, storming, and norming stages until new working relationships are established and maximum performance is again achieved. Communities need to be reassured that organizations which cycle back to "norming" or "storming" stages are participating in normal organizational behavior.

ADJOURNING: As the name implies, this marks the final "all good things must come to an end" stage. Adjournment is not failure, but rather the normal expectation of an organization (or community) that has served its purpose. While adjournment may be the logical or appropriate action, it should always be a conscious choice not the result of apathy or lack of development capacity.

We don't normally think about communities in an organizational sense, but they also were formed for a purpose and go through the various organizational stages or cycles. In their book, *Enlightened Leadership, Getting to the Heart of Change*, authors Ed Oakley and Doug Krug (1994) state;

"*Recognizing the importance and need for change is the mark of a healthy, renewing person or organization. This ability to be flexible and highly adaptable requires an attitude of openness and opportunity, rather than a mindset dominated by problems and fear. We call this renewing attitude change-friendly.*" (p. 39)

This same thought extends to communities. Communities are, after all, organizations that were formed to serve common needs. Ghost towns are not organizational anomalies, but rather examples of communities that served their purpose. Mining towns ceased to exist when mines closed. Some factory towns have met the same fate. Towns built along the railroads were spaced at eight to ten mile distances to feed wood burning engines.

When technology or economic opportunities changed, the original reasons for forming many communities was drastically altered. Some communities found new purpose and continue to thrive while others vanished because they fulfilled their original organizational functions. While nostalgia may cause us to long for the good old days, the reality is that communities and organizations are purpose driven. They both need to have reasons to exist. When the reason or need no longer exists, the community or organization will eventually cease to function unless it is imbued with a new purpose.

WHERE ARE YOU NOW?

In discussing the success of an organization, Ed Oakley and Doug Krug (1994) suggest:

"Change is a factor that every organization must accept, so how effectively change is implemented becomes more and more critical to the long-term success of an organization." (p 26).

Understanding the organizational cycle may help your community or organization identify where it is now and help it plan to move to a more productive stage of development, ensuring long-term success (or allow it to exit gracefully knowing it has served its purpose). Again, this should be a conscious choice, not the unfortunate result of apathy or lack of development capacity.

TO PAY OR NOT TO PAY...
THAT IS THE QUESTION

As the need for organizational capacity grows, a community or organization will eventually begin discussing hiring part-time or full-time staff. Resource providers are often asked if it is better to hire someone who is already trained and ready to hit the ground running or to find a local person and invest in training them. This is another question that can be answered in more than one way. Your organization will have to decide what resources it has available, both immediate and long-range, to determine the level of financial commitment you can make to staffing.

If your budget is modest, you may need to start with a part-time employee and that suggests a local person. First, however, you need to ensure you have the financial commitment to provide the type of training necessary for the development of your organization or community. Smaller communities often choose this option and expand the job to full-time as resources become available.

If your budget allows you to start with a full-time person, you will need to weigh the benefits of hiring a professional developer compared to employing a local individual. Both choices have pros and cons. Visit with your local and regional resource providers and other communities that have hired staff to help you evaluate your options.

Once there is staff, a community has a tendency to say, "That's what we hired them for - I'm staying home". I cannot stress enough that hiring staff does not relieve the committees, boards, and volunteers of their need to participate. I recommend a group go through an exercise similar to the one listed below to differentiate which functions the paid staff will perform, functions the board will assume, and functions that volunteers will undertake.

Again, using a simple matrix, list the major functions or duties of the organization along the vertical side under columns headed Board, Staff, and Volunteers (you may want to include a column for Resource Providers to identify where you need, and can anticipate receiving, outside participation). The only rule is that staff cannot be the answer to every activity. You will find this tool especially important when you hire staff, as role clarification is the biggest challenge of a new organization or one making the change from a volunteer-base to a part-time or full-time staff. *(Please see example on next page.)*

Funding for staff and other administrative costs, such as office space and supplies will be a major consideration. There are many funding models for development from which to choose based on whether city staff is employed, and the type of organization is public/private, quasi-governmental, not-for-profit or for-profit. Funding operations and administration often requires multiple sources since some funds have restrictions on their use.

Here is an abbreviated sample:

ACTIVITY	BOARD	STAFF	VOLUNTEERS	RESOURCE PROVIDERS
Spokesperson to media	Board President	Staff is secondary	Refer to staff	
Information responses	Any board member	Staff is primary		
Project completion	Board may assist	Staff coordinates	Volunteers complete	Technical Assistance
Fundraising	Board responsibility	Staff should only be in a support role - not responsible for fundraising	Volunteers support and help complete	
Specific activity	May be involved in a specific activity	Staff coordinates	This is where your skills database is useful	Know your resource providers and what assistance they can offer

Employees should not be responsible for fund-raising, although they certainly may be involved in grant writing, if the organization makes that part of the job description. The problem with employees undertaking fundraising efforts for the organization is the perception that all fund requests are benefiting the employee salaries. This misperception often results in funders or donors declining involvement with the projects and can jeopardize the credibility of the employee requesting donations. Requiring an employee to find and maintain organizational funding also removes the organization's board from upholding its responsibility to the organization. It is important for an organization or community to realize that employees may not be long-term as they move on to other opportunities or leave for any number of reasons including health. The ongoing commitment to the organization and control of its finances should remain with the board.

Board members should be active supporters of the organization beyond just attending board meetings. Active participation in organizational projects, planning sessions, learning opportunities and networking are all appropriate board functions. The DDD/TTT test can be a useful tool to help existing and prospective board members verbalize their commitment. DDD stands for Doer, Donor, Door Opener and the TTT stands for Time, Treasure and Talent. You may find the following pledge form a useful tool.

BOARD OF DIRECTORS - PARTICIPATION PLEDGE

Each board member needs to ***actively*** support the organization. ***This pledge helps identify the specific duties each member is willing to undertake this year.*** Read the role categories and examples. Please be specific about the project(s) and activities you support by filling in the far right column and signing the pledge at the bottom. You may choose more than one way to participate and all help will be appreciated. **THANK YOU** for your contribution to the board and these activities.

ROLE	EXPLANATION	EXAMPLE	MY SPECIFIC ACTIVITY
DOER	Volunteer your time for specific projects	Set up tables for meetings	
DONOR	CASH support	Cash for grant matching funds	
DOOR OPENER	Network within the community and beyond the community to achieve needed resources	Speak about this program at another organization	
TIME	Similar to DOER - donate staff and family time	10 hours of staff time donated to researching funding opportunities	
TREASURE	Similar to DONOR - may share non-cash valuables for project support	Donate merchandise for drawings or prizes, or donate items needed by the organization, i.e. computer equipment	
TALENT	Volunteer specific talents to support activities	Use computer knowledge to set up organizational database	

_____   _____

(Print Name)   (Date)

_____

(Signature)

As you can see, it is very simple yet makes a public commitment, and gives the staff a reference for specific assistance. Every board member should be able to fill in at least one category. This form also can be useful when recruiting new board members as it helps them clarify organizational expectations and allows them to state what their contributions may be.

BUSINESS ASSISTANCE CAPACITY

When discussing economic organizational development, you need to assess your business community to determine what types of business assistance are needed and what your organization has the capacity to provide. The basic business assistance needs are:

- **Recruitment** Attracting new businesses to your community, which includes having land to build on, or buildings available for occupancy, and local financial assistance or incentives.

- **Existing Business Assistance** Helping with retention and expansion opportunities including employee training and local financial or technical assistance.

- **Business Transfer** As business owners plan for retirement, can you keep the business in your community by helping facilitate ownership transfers with technical or financial assistance?

- **Start-up and Entrepreneurial Assistance** Growing local businesses is a proven development tool for many communities and usually requires intensive technical assistance and appropriate financial assistance.

Once you have determined your local assistance capabilities you can network with external development partners to find further assistance for businesses. Every organization and community possesses different internal skills and external partners. Knowing what is available now will be beneficial later when an opportunity arises.

RECOGNIZE THE
ORGANIZATIONAL CAPACITY

Understand the organizational network in your community. Occasionally plan a forum with representatives of all local development organizations to share the big picture of the community and its development options. Include regional and state resource providers to keep current on their programs and abilities to assist your endeavors. Look for opportunities for group collaboration; for gaps that need addressing, and most of all, look for successes to celebrate.

INFRASTRUCTURE CAPACITY

Infrastructure capacity is vital to any development program.   Just what do we mean by infrastructure? According to Merriam-Webster online the definitions include:

1. The underlying foundation or basic framework (as of a system or organization)
2. The permanent installations required for military purposes
3. The system of public works of a country, state, or region; also: the resources (as personnel, buildings, or equipment) required for an activity (www.webster.com/dictionary)

When broadly defined as in the examples above, community infrastructure includes your human capacity for personnel, your organizational capacity, and by inference the financial capacity to ensure ongoing support.

Commonly infrastructure is considered tangible items - the physical responses needed for community or project development. This includes land, buildings, equipment, and supporting systems such as streets, sidewalks, water, wastewater, power sources, telecommunications, and other facility needs.

Infrastructure is often the jurisdiction of the local elected officials and city councils or village boards are historically conservators of public funds, carefully watching and evaluating all requests for expenditures. They need compelling reasons to expend limited community resources on infrastructure. Well-planned projects help bridge local officials' need for justification of expenses and the community's need for infrastructure.

In *Clues to Rural Community Survival* (1998), authors Vicki Luther and Milan Wall state:

"*Thriving rural communities understand the importance of physical infrastructures - such as streets, sidewalks, water systems, sewage treatment plants - and efforts are made to maintain and improve them.*" (p. 15)

Community infrastructure includes housing for residents and employees, and social infrastructure such as schools and medical care, child care, and recreational facilities. A well-developed community can offer all of these amenities to meet the needs of its population, or is planning how to meet the needs to ensure its future growth.

Organizational infrastructure is the equipment that allows the organization to operate smoothly and achieve its goals. Development organizations often set goals that the community infrastructure does not support and forget to plan how to make the needed infrastructure possible. Remember Jack's earlier comment about not building a bowling alley if you want to attract a baseball team.

Economic development infrastructure has specific needs. According to James Christenson and Jerry Robinson, Jr. (1989),

"*While development as improvement tends to focus more on the social and psychological transformations in societies and communities, development as growth involves technological and economic transformation. Development as growth focuses on economic prosperity.*" (p. 9).

Any planning for economic development within the community needs to include assessing and then addressing infrastructure issues. What are the infrastructure requirements of your planned economic development project, and the ancillary requirements created by the project? Do you have the organizational and financial capacity to build whatever level of infrastructure is required? Does your project timeline allow for construction?

If your economic development strategy is business recruitment, you will need land, buildings, utilities, public works, easements, accesses, and a laundry list of other items. If you successfully recruitment a business or businesses, do you have a readily available and local trained workforce to meet the needs of the company or companies? Do you have enough safe, affordable housing to entice additional employees to move to your community? Do you have the necessary childcare facilities and school classroom capacity to welcome additional children to the community?

If your strategy is to assist existing or start-up businesses, many of the same questions will need to be answered. These businesses may also need land or buildings, additional utilities, more water or wastewater access, and other community resources. If the companies are creating or adding jobs, the issues of available housing, child care, schools, trained workforce and other concerns will need to be addressed.

When thinking about infrastructure, you need to analyze more than the traditional systems. Technology infrastructure, or the lack thereof, is truly "*tearing down the traditional boundaries between nations, economies, individuals, the boundaries dividing the haves from the have-nots.*", according to Ed Oakley and Doug Krug in their book *Enlightened Leadership, Getting to the Heart of Change* (1994, p.7).

Technology is changing so fast that it is considered a constant financial and infrastructure development challenge. The best part about technology is that the jobs created are not necessarily place dependent. The old economic development mantra of "location, location, location" is not necessarily true anymore. You don't have to be near an interstate, near your office, or even near your customer, which opens up a world of opportunities for those organizations and communities willing to invest in technology infrastructure.

ONGOING INFRASTRUCTURE CAPACITY

Infrastructure capacity is not a one-time effort. In addition to the original construction, finances are necessary for ongoing updates and maintenance. Equipment gets outdated, roads need to be resurfaced or widened, buildings need to be adapted for current needs, and water systems need to be expanded; just to name a few examples. Infrastructure not only requires, it demands, constant capacity inputs, and those inputs require **FINANCIAL CAPACITY.**

FINANCIAL CAPACITY

As federal and state resources and budgets tighten, it is more important than ever to maintain local control of financial capacity. Local financing can be used to fund projects thereby eliminating the red tape involved with grant awards. Local funding proves a more personal commitment to a project as the community rallies to raise capital for local or regional needs.

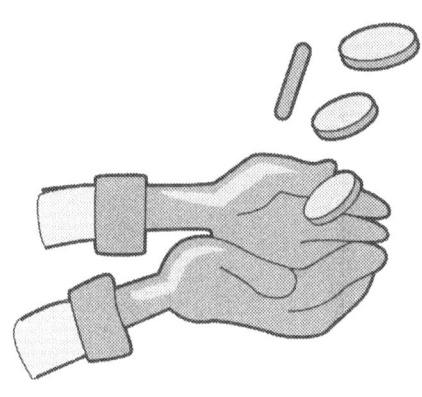 Local money also can be the necessary match required for many grant applications. Even philanthropic foundations are funding fewer projects; especially those foundations set up to protect capital and make awards or grants only from the interest earned. These types of foundations often require more local match to help stretch their grant resources.

It is time for communities and organizations to move away from the dependency model of development where grants are awarded according to how poor or needy a community or organization is. We need to move to the capacity model where we prove we are capable of completing meaningful projects and have a community or organizational history that warrants the trust of the granting entity. For now the dependency model is still the basis for many state and federal programs with requirements to meet certain LMI (low to moderate income) thresholds. These awards may be coupled with consideration of the commitment (match) of the community and the capacity of the applicant to administer the grant and complete the project so building that financial and organizational capacity now is still important to grant applications.

The capacity for a community or organization to utilize the grant or award offered is critical to both the granting entity that needs a record of project completion and the community that needs to establish organizational credibility. For example, one community received a generous financial donation to construct a swimming pool from a former resident but once it was built, it could not be used because the community did not have the capacity or funds to manage the costs of operation. The donor's expectation of endowing a wonderful legacy became a community liability because the capacity had not been developed for the project's long-term continuation.

Once again we see the value of strategic planning for both long-range and short-term considerations. In their book *Designing Development Strategies in Small Towns,* Glen Pulver and David Dodson (1992), comment:

> *"The rural landscape is littered with communities that have made large and unsuccessful investments - in industrial parks, promotional campaigns, airstrips, and tourist facilities - without first mapping where they stand in a competitive environment. Neighboring communities often mimic each other and fail. As the competition for*

public and private investment dollars grows, the cost of such well-intentioned but ill-informed ventures will soar, and the value of grounding community action in a strategic assessment of strengths, vulnerabilities, and options will be confirmed." (p. 3)

It is important to understand that most projects have a financial consideration. Sometimes the available finances or the ability to build additional financial capacity determine the goals set or projects accomplished while the lack of financial capacity (as in the swimming pool example) negates a wonderful community opportunity.

I heard a speaker suggest that local financial investment is the "rent" we all should pay for the services we receive from our community. Even recognizing that many services are tax supported, the community as a whole offers additional amenities and types of support that are not financially based. So how does a community or organization plan for financial development of both the organization and business community? There are probably as many financing options as there are development groups, but here are a couple of ideas for your consideration:

- **Local Funding – In Kind**

   Whenever discussing how to finance projects, it is important to understand in-kind financial opportunities and responsibilities. In-kind is the use of labor, supplies, and resources. Some grant programs will allow in-kind as part or all of a community's or organization's matching requirement. In-kind also is a way to describe the local volunteer projects that happen without any outside financial resources. Habitat for Humanity depends on hours of in-kind contributions from its many volunteers.

If using in-kind, you will need to know what type of documentation is required, how the in-kind is used as match for other funds, and what is an acceptable in-kind donation. For example, some programs will only allow labor if the person volunteering is employed to perform the same service for a fee for others. A licensed electrician might wire your office and be counted as an in-kind contribution, but the nice landlord may not be an eligible in-kind match for performing the same volunteer service.

- **Local Funding - Fundraising**

Traditional fundraising techniques are a good way to finance a local project, especially if the community or organization doesn't need to raise large sums of money. It also is a good way to raise the amount needed for local match if you are requesting grant assistance. Communities or organizations wanting to use this strategy are encouraged to turn "fundraising" into "fun"draising. Be creative and have fun. Include as many different groups as you can in your effort to gain more community support for the project.

Some states offer a tax credit program that facilitates local fundraising efforts. Donors to qualified projects receive a partial credit for their donation on their state tax. These tax credit programs are state administered and have varying conditions for use. Check with your state to see if they have a similar community development program.

- **Local Funding - Revolving Loan Funds**

    These are earmarked business expansion and development funds generated from a variety of sources, including specific loans or grants to establish funds, the recapture and re-use of community business incentives, private local investments, and local taxes used to establish business development funds. There are distinct advantages to establishing a local pool of money that can be used to leverage other financing. The money is controlled locally so can offer more flexibility to meet the needs of businesses. Local oversight of the funding also instills commitment of the community or organization to further ensure the loan applicant's success by providing necessary technical and business assistance.

- **Local Funding - Investment Clubs**

    As communities and organizations look for ways to increase control over projects, forming a local investment club may be worth considering.

I have worked with several communities that have successfully funded or helped fund local development projects through an investment club. These clubs raise private funds and the use is strictly dictated by the club's own membership and guidelines. The investment clubs are meant to be for-profit but usually are willing to assume some local risk. These funds are frequently earmarked as the local match for a grant, or to help provide down payments or other financial assistance for a project.

One community started its club with a $1,000 buy-in and an agreement to invest $100 monthly. They had 15 members sign up the first day and immediately had $15,000 to use for community and economic development projects. As they add to that on a monthly basis, earn interest on their investments, and receive loan repayments; the pool will continue to grow, offer financing options to the community, and eventually will provide return on investment to the members.

Another community started its club with a $500 initial investment and a $50 monthly pledge. Although their pool will grow more slowly, they feel they will attract more members. Every club has the right to decide what rules will apply. Because these clubs are legal entities you need to be sure you have good information and legal advice before starting an investment club.

Investment club money is sometimes referred to as "patient" money as the group can set its own interest and repayment terms, often allowing a project or business to use the funds for a period of time before any repayment is scheduled.

- **Local Funding - Private Investors or Angels**

    Some communities are lucky enough to have people who are willing to invest directly in the community by assisting businesses or projects. Project assistance often comes in the form of a benevolent gift from a current or former resident in memory of a loved one. One community recently received such a gift from a former resident who generously donated a large sum of money to build a new community center. His reason for the gift was that he never forgot his hometown.

    Equally important, but usually less public, are those people who are willing to give financial assistance to a local business. This may be in the form of an outright grant, a long-term loan, a loan with no interest, down payment assistance, or other creative ways to help meet a business need. These investors may or may not live in your community. They may be people who have successfully gone on with their careers and who have altruistic motives for helping their hometown. Matching these willing local investors with local needs is a win-win for your community. Your organizational capacity will be important to networking the businesses and investors since angel investors often want to be anonymous or at least receive minimal publicity.

- **Local Funding - Endowments and Foundations**

No discussion of financial capacity would be complete without mentioning the ability of local foundations or endowments to finance local projects. As organizations and communities plan for future financial capacity, either adding to existing foundations or starting foundations is an excellent way to encourage local investment and charitable giving.

Some professionals and consultants warn that the coming intergenerational transfer of wealth may be the largest in American history. If communities and organizations are not positioned to offer an investment opportunity and encourage philanthropic giving, the wealth will leave the community following the steps of the heirs and residents who have moved on to other locales.

Endowments that are tied to projects help ensure these projects' ongoing sustainability. If local financial capacity is not adequate for a project, foundations and endowments also may serve as matching funds on grant requests thereby offering communities and organizations the ability to generate outside funds.

- **Public Funding - Local**

  Communities have a limited ability to raise funds by enacting certain local taxes. Most of these taxes have very restrictive uses and the subject of more taxes is never popular. Each community will have to decide what its local tax capacity is and how they want to allocate the available resources. The willingness of the local citizens to invest in their community and its future can send a powerful message.

  In Nebraska, there is a Local Option Municipal Economic Development Sales Tax that communities can enact. It requires a vote of the community and has some restrictions. More information about this program can be found on the Nebraska Department of Economic Development website www.neded.org.

  One small community recently passed this tax even though it was only estimated to raise $8,000 a year for economic development purposes. They felt it was a good message to send, and a starting place to build local commitment and capacity.

  A small company in another state was looking for a place to expand their business and through networking heard about this small town in southwestern Nebraska willing to tax itself even for such a modest sum. The company chose this small community for its expansion and has created about 20 jobs. This all happened before the community ever realized any of the proceeds of the new tax.

- **Public Funding - Regional, State and Federal**

  Although we have been talking primarily about building local financial capacity, we need to acknowledge the regional, state and federal public funding assistance that can enable a community to gain capacity. There are many available programs and they are subject to change with federal and state budget constraints and political winds. Normally, if a community meets certain criteria they can find assistance with housing and public infrastructure. There also is public funding available to communities to help businesses that are creating or saving jobs. Check with your regional, state, and federal development partners to learn about the funding sources available.

FINANCIAL CAPACITY INVESTING

Financial capacity is necessary to facilitate growth in a community, maintain local control of development and prepare for future development opportunities. As noted in the previous section, there are many forms of financial capacity. Emphasis has been placed on various forms of <u>local</u> financial capacity and funds because these are where communities have impact, control, and opportunity to build financial capacity.

Each community or organization will need to find the best mix of local funding sources to ensure the success of their current project, and also the ongoing viability of their organization, or community.

The more local options available, the greater the chances are for success when an opportunity is presented.

With the exception of certain grant programs, outside money rarely is available until there has been local investment. Also, learn to think of all financers (whether local or imported resources) as *investors*. Be prepared to state what their Return on Investment (ROI) will be for assisting you.

DOSES OF DEVELOPMENT

These are small development efforts and ideas that might help jump-start your organizational or community efforts. You can also find books on development at the library, many resource providers have books or booklets on development ideas, and the Internet has a wealth of information on the topic. Following are some of my favorites:

- **Flags for late hour merchants**

    If your community's retail stores traditionally closes the store by 5 or 6 p.m. during the week, or open only until noon on Saturday, you might consider this idea I overheard at a conference. The speaker said he was from a town specializing in stores that cater to the unemployed as these retail outlets were never open during hours that working people could shop. A community in another state solved this by having some merchants extend hours one night a week. Those stores that agreed to remain open until 8 p.m. on Thursday night flew community flags all week to let the public know that they participated in the later hours program. While it started with just two or three stores, others began staying open later, too.

The cafes and eateries in the community noticed an increase in business on Thursdays as people grabbed a bite to eat while they were out shopping. This was a small change for the community, but eventually word spread to neighboring communities and the "late hour" community became a Thursday night hot spot, often attracting women from throughout the area for a girl's night out, which translated into additional shopping and dinner customers.

- **Second story window treatments**
  Many communities have downtown buildings with second stories (or more). As the demand for downtown space changed, these floors often remain unused. Your community could benefit greatly from giving the impression that these floors are occupied by cleaning windows, hanging curtains, and placing small decorative items within the windowsill. Of course this needs to be regularly maintained or it will quickly become apparent that the tattered curtains only frame empty rooms. Some communities are successfully converting empty second story floors into desirable, sometimes high-end, apartments and housing units, which helps resolve the need for additional housing and creates a more viable community atmosphere.

  In Unionville, Mo., a small town without a motel, an enterprising couple renovated second floor apartments and offers them for rent as overnight accommodations. Overnight guests now have a local motel-type option meaning they also spend more money locally for meals, gas, and other purchases.

- **Empty buildings**

    Almost every town, no matter how large or small, has an empty retail or commercial building at some time. Following are some clever ideas other communities have used to more positively market their downtowns.

    o A large sign in the window stating " *Future home of* ____ *(help fill in the blank)".* This encouraged local people to help think of ways to fill the building or to spread the word that the building was available.

    o Use the empty windows to showcase items from other businesses in the community. For example, one town's furniture store, clothing store, and florist combined to dress the windows in an empty store and placed signs near each item identifying the local stores that carried the products. They had fun displaying their products in this joint venture and began cross-selling merchandise.

    o Local craft/home business display. Home-based businesses might arrange to display local products in empty storefront windows. Again signage featuring contact information of the local businesses helps prospective buyers find the business and purchase products.

- **Be a mentor**

This simple, but effective suggestion helps assimilate new residents into communities or committees' planning and organizing projects. Invite a new neighbor to accompany you to a meeting. Visit with neighbors or new residents about ongoing projects. Share your time and help build the local human capacity.

- **Find a mentor**

On the other hand, if you want to volunteer but don't know where to start, find people who already are involved in projects you admire, or an organization that interests you, and ask them if you can accompany them to find out more about participating. I have never yet seen any community that has too many volunteers.

- **Become a "sister city"**

Offer your community's expertise to another town undertaking similar projects, or working with similar organizational development issues. If you are contemplating a project or establishing a new organization, find a community that has already experienced success and ask for their assistance. Visit that community and learn about their efforts firsthand. You may not want to duplicate their project or organization exactly because you want to do what fits your community, but you can learn from their process and adapt the project or organization to your specific needs.

- **Each one bring one - build your volunteer base**

  Using tools such as the "name game" found earlier in the book, ask each member of the organization or project committee to identify and personally bring one volunteer or prospective member to the next meeting. Friends or acquaintances that invite individuals often experience a greater response rate than the "you all come" invitations typically posted around town or inserted into newspapers. Personal invitation usually fosters enthusiasm for and commitment to the current project.

- **Volunteer for one specific duty**

  Don't wait to be asked to participate. When you see a project or organizational opportunity, volunteer for one specific duty. You will help build human and organizational capacity. You also will have greater control over what you choose to do and when you do it, and avoid being trapped in the "volunteer for life" syndrome.

- **Attend a networking meeting in your region or state**

  The value of networking cannot be stressed enough. The world will not come to your community saying, "Have I got a deal for you". Meeting your resource providers, getting involved in regional solutions, and finding out about helpful community programs all require travel outside the city limits. Take advantage of the available workshops, seminars, and other training opportunities. Build capacity by familiarizing the resource providers and regional representatives with your community or organization.

These ideas and examples can be initiated in your community or organization with little or no expense, yet make a powerful statement about your community's willingness to improve and adapt. Once you have completed some of these ideas, you will learn and adapt others as you network to develop and build local capacity.

TRIED AND TRUE

There are many excellent examples of all facets of development. I have chosen to feature a few examples of communities that have made choices that fit their unique needs and built local capacity to reach their goals. However, I caution that you need to adapt these examples to your own community or organization.   It has been said that imitation is the greatest form of flattery. Take the best of these ideas and imitate them - adding your own local touch or twist to make them uniquely your own.

COOPERATION AND COALITIONS

Much has been written and said about the power of cooperation and coalition building as many small communities no longer have the population mass or financial resources to "go it alone". This example is a group that overcame political boundaries by crossing county lines and including non-traditional partners in their new effort.

A few years ago a small regional power cooperative helped start a grassroots economic development effort for its service territory, which included Furnas and Harlan counties, Nebraska. Coalition building for this new regional effort was accomplished through a series of small steps. First, a steering committee was formed, made up of representatives of many agencies and resource providers that serve the two counties, as well as community-minded citizens. This group identified common issues and new ways to incorporate the "co-opetition" mentioned earlier in the book.

The steering committee met for several months to plan a two-county town hall meeting. The local consolidated school was chosen as a neutral setting since it was in a rural area, not any specific community. Also the school's consolidation efforts had already drawn some people to work together beyond the traditional town borders.

At the meeting, resource providers presented information about the local and state economy. They used the "Rusty Bucket" process to get people thinking about the area's economic inputs and leakages. These inputs and leakages were then categorized and committees were formed around various topics. Volunteers were grouped according to their interest in specific topics. Facilitated discussions helped develop committee work plans. Resource providers shared information about appropriate and available resources as committees drew up their plans. Several follow-up meetings were held to introduce the committees to additional resource providers and panels of citizens from other towns that had resolved some similar local issues.

The informal partnership grew, attracted some modest financial resources, and decided to become official. The governor attended the ceremony marking the signing of interlocal agreements that formed the official partnership and the **Furnas Harlan Partnership** was born. Getting all communities in the two county area to cooperate through interlocal agreements set the stage for the new regional effort in a distressed area of the state.

Although the Furnas Harlan Partnership started as a volunteer organization with several strong committees, the group has secured enough funding to hire part-time staff and continues to make progress in realizing regional goals. The Partnership recently received grant funding that will allow it to provide education on business transfers, start-ups, and entrepreneurship. They continue to build their own organizational capacity and the developmental capacity of the region through cooperation and coalition building.

A NEW COMMUNITY

As residential areas experience growth, some investors are building "planned communities" complete with parks and other amenities. The Weyerhaeuser Company, a company known for logging and lumber, developed two such planned communities. Weyerhaeuser is planning to develop 9,300 homes and apartments between the two developments and projects a population of 21,000 residents.

The first, **Meridian Campus** near **Lacey, Wash**. is a 1,153 acre planned community one hour south of Seattle. The community boasts a wildlife preserve running through the acreage as a corridor between the Nisqually Wildlife Refuge and Tolmie State Park. Bald eagles, deer, raccoons, and other mammals frequent the hiking and biking trails in Meridian Campus. Additionally, there are two elementary schools and a middle school located in the community.

The second, **Northwest Landing** near **DuPont, Wash**, also is about one hour from Seattle. DuPont was incorporated in 1951 and has approximately 5,300 residents. The area received recognition on the National Register of Historic Places in 1987. The community of DuPont has a long and varied history. It was a company town from 1906 until 1951 when residents were allowed to purchase their homes. Adjacent to the community was a dynamite manufacturing plant owned by DuPont. When the plant closed in 1976, DuPont sold the 3,200 acres to the Weyerhaeuser Company which is now developing the site into the mixed use planned community within the city limits of DuPont. The design calls for 1,000 acres zoned for industrial, office, and commercial development. Another 1,000 acres is planned for residential neighborhoods and 1,000 acres have been reserved for open space. When Northwest Landing is complete, it will feature homes for approximately 12,100 people and create jobs for 20,800. Northwest Landing boasts about its small-town character and homes with porches.

These two examples, and all other planned communities, offer residents unusual opportunities to participate in organizations and to help build local community capacity. With little or no organizational infrastructure in place, it will be interesting to observe how volunteers and leaders evolve to meet community needs.

PARTNERING WITH RESOURCES

Ord, **Neb,** has gone from a sleepy little village to a development "hot spot" in about five years. How did utilizing resource providers help this community develop capacity?

In the 1990s, Ord lost 8.5 percent of its population and the county was experiencing similar losses. In March of 2000, the Ord Area Chamber of Commerce invited representatives of the Nebraska Department of Economic Development (DED) and Nebraska Public Power District (NPPD) to a town hall meeting. Approximately 60 people attended the meeting and an economic development sub-committee of the Chamber of Commerce was formed.

Several follow-up meetings held with DED and NPPD staff through June of 2000 helped the local citizens understand what resources were available and what they needed to accomplish at the local level to access state and federal assistance. The meetings also stressed what needed to be done to build the local capacity to plan and execute programs. The planning committee included representatives of the Ord Area Chamber of Commerce, city of Ord, Valley County Board of Supervisors, and the Greater Loup Valley Activities, Inc. who met regularly to learn about their economy and about other communities' successes.

The timing was right to merge an existing chamber position into a joint chamber and economic development position, so the city of Ord and Valley County entered into an interlocal agreement creating the Valley County Economic Development Board. They, along with the Ord Chamber of Commerce and Greater Loup Valley Activities, Inc., joined resources and hired a full-time economic development director/chamber manager. They have since added several staff to coordinate specific projects.

Since that time, Ord has gone on to receive local, regional, state and national recognition for its development activities. The community has implemented a holistic approach to development and is not focusing on just one segment. Projects have included successful industry attraction, business retention, health care expansions, downtown renovations, housing, entrepreneurship, and youth retention. The economic development staff also has been instrumental in sharing information with the community about other capacity building programs, such as the local investment club that allows people to invest in their community and help leverage other resources.

While Ord's citizens are definitely the success story, involving resource providers early in the process helped establish a firm foundation for their efforts. The planning committee and, later the economic development organization, was able to benefit from the resource providers' knowledge of appropriate trainings, programs, and additional resource providers to meet the community needs. The community has rightfully earned the Nebraska Showcase Community award.

A NEW PURPOSE

How do some communities find a new purpose when they reach that inevitable part of the organizational cycle called "adjourning"? You are probably familiar with stories about Branson, Mo., the new home of country music or Leavenworth, Wash., the Bavarian village with no Bavarian heritage. Many communities have built new identities around a product or festival to help revitalize their area. Pella, Iowa, is famous for its Dutch heritage and Tulip Festival. Sturgis, SD, is a mecca for motorcycle enthusiasts. Other communities also have found a new purpose or reason to exist.

I'd like to share the story of **Port Gamble, Wash**, an example of successful reinvention. The sawmill and village, in which my Mother was raised, was founded in 1853. By 1879, Port Gamble was the largest sawmill town in the entire country, not just the northwest. When the sawmill closed in 1995, Port Gamble had established itself as the oldest continuously operating sawmill in North America.

More than 200 employees worked at the Pope and Talbot mill during the 1920s. Multiply the number of employees by their families (my grandparents raised 12 children) and you can see why the town thrived. The population was recorded as 326 by 1870 and peaked at 500 in the early 1920s. The town's beautiful hotel featured impressive furniture that had been delivered by ship around Cape Horn. It also supported a church, school, company store and several streets of houses. Houses were assigned based on the job one had at the mill so as workers got promoted, they moved into larger and nicer homes.

The self-supporting town offered everything its mill workers and families needed through its company-owned store, hospital, and even morgue. Homes were located close to the mill enabling workers to easily walk to and from their jobs. With the advent of the affordable car in the 1920s, workers moved away from company-owned homes into homes of their own, and the town began to lose population.

By the 1960s, Port Gamble was dying. The hotel was torn down, the school demolished, and some homes sat empty and abandoned. At some point in 1960, the town's owners (Olympic Property Group) undertook a successful effort to get the unique sawmill village on the National Historic Register.

Today, the village still showcases New England Victorian-style homes, and St. Paul's Church (where my parents were married) has become a wedding destination site. According to Port Gamble's website, couples can be married in the historic St. Paul's church or the adjoining pavilion. A church wedding is priced at $250 per hour with a minimum of three hours, and the pavilion rents for $2,000 a day.

Entrepreneurs are once again filling the homes with quaint shops and artist studios. The current population is less than 100, but the community is, once again, growing its population, and is a tourist destination that offers a variety of markets, antique shops, festivals, and artists' offerings. The Olympic Property Group (OPG) is redeveloping the community with an emphasis on being a family-friendly hamlet.

The idea is for Port Gamble to be a wonderful place in which to live and raise families, and where visitors are welcome to enjoy a step back in time. OPG also is developing some land holdings into housing developments and working with the public to plan a long-range development strategy for the area. The Group estimates that with the right kind of development, Port Gamble's area population could be near 1,000 in the next five to ten years.

Not far from Port Gamble is another example of a community that continues to find new purpose - **Poulsbo, Wash.** Scandinavian immigrants, mainly Norwegians settled Poulsbo (pronounced Paul's Bo) in the 1880s. In fact, the primary language was Norwegian until World War II brought an influx of new residents that nearly tripled the community's and changed the dominant language to English.

The 2000 census showed a population of 6,813 in Poulsbo. By 2005 it had grown to 7,450 (and approximately 30,000 counting everyone with a Poulsbo address) with additional growth predicted.

Like many communities, Poulsbo has experienced growth spurts and lean times. In the community's first 25 years, it included a post office, school, church, orphanage, hotel, newspaper (which still operates today), a telephone company, bank, and a codfish company.

During its earliest history, water was the primary mode of travel with the 18-mile trip to and from Seattle made in small steamboats called the "mosquito fleet". The fleet served Poulsbo and other locations along Liberty Bay (originally known as Dog Fish Bay) and Puget Sound. The boats carried passengers and freight from Seattle to the small villages and delivered produce to the Pike Place Market in Seattle. (My Dad and his family were among those regular riders taking products to the Market via the mosquito fleet.)

Many commercial fishermen who lived in the Poulsbo area left each season for the Alaskan fishing grounds. The local lifestyles truly revolved around salt water with the close proximity of the Pacific Ocean and tidal waters of both Puget Sound and Hood's Canal within easy travel. State-owned ferries leaving from Bainbridge Island still offer commuters the fastest transportation to jobs and other destinations in the Seattle area.

Growing up in or near Poulsbo and Port Gamble provided a great sense of the history of Kitsap County even as shopping and community growth declined while businesses tried to compete with larger nearby towns in the region, and even with Seattle. In the 1950s, Poulsbo chose to address the loss of retail and sense of community by emphasizing their Norwegian heritage. They started with a downtown beautification project that involved renaming Dog Fish Bay to Liberty Bay, revamping the pier area to include parking and a waterfront park (now home to many events), and some stores began to be decorated with rosemaling (a traditional Norwegian art form).

Today the area's three marinas often welcome visiting boats and yachts as tourists come to see the picturesque storefronts, browse the unique gift shops, and enjoy the variety of food offerings (including the famous Poulsbo Bread). All this is coupled with the beautiful bay set against the backdrop of the Olympic Mountains.

Not wanting to just be a tourist mecca, Poulsbo also worked to become a leader in providing publicly-owned fiber-optic infrastructure providing expanded employment options. In many ways, Poulsbo continues to find new purposes while keeping one eye on maintaining its rich heritage and nickname of "Little Norway".

CAPTURING FINANCIAL ASSETS

Aurora, Neb., has done an exceptional job of building financial capacity and community cohesiveness. The community also has made a significant commitment to advancing technology.

Aurora's "overnight success" is actually the culmination of more than 40 years of financial commitment to the community. By emphasizing quality business and community life, Aurora has created building blocks that include affordable housing, a strong educational system, quality labor, local business support, and tourism investment, in addition to undertaking traditional business expansion and business recruitment strategies employed by most successful communities. With the help of several existing businesses, Aurora has invested in a high-tech business incubator that has attracted new businesses to the community. They have joined their chamber and economic development efforts and hired a full-time director and additional staff to coordinate the variety of projects and programs underway.

Aurora is the proud home of the Plainsman Museum and Edgerton Explorit Center – a hands-on science facility dedicated to the pioneering work of Nebraska native "Doc" Harold Edgerton, that features interactive science exhibits and learning opportunities for teachers and for students. Aurora has many other wonderful public buildings and a beautiful business area centered around the courthouse. Several major manufacturers have located in the area and Aurora's economic diversity ranges from agriculture to hi-tech industry.

Private contributions, rather than tax dollars, have built a substantial portion of Aurora's infrastructure. Additionally, more than 30 community organizations depend heavily on volunteerism and work cooperatively with the business community, city and county to achieve local goals. Aurora's website lists 15 foundations, trusts, and non-profit organizations impacting the community with more than $30 million in assets. Many foundations and trusts provide scholarships and funding for local projects. According to additional information I found on their community website, 71 different entities offer educational scholarship opportunities, ranging from $400 to $3,200.

Aurora's community-wide strategic plan involved input from hundreds of residents helping to determine the needs and opportunities for the area. While many communities struggle with the concept of local philanthropy, Aurora has become a model for what can happen when a community builds the financial capacity to control its own destiny and then adds in the extra element of local cooperation.

INFRASTRUCTURE

Infrastructure is an ongoing need for communities. Maintenance, upgrades, and newer technology require communities to constantly review and revise their infrastructure capacity just to maintain the status quo. If they are fortunate in attracting a major employer or a housing development, they will need to expand infrastructure.

As noted earlier, infrastructure often is defined as those tangible items needed for community or project development. This includes land, buildings, equipment, and support systems, such as streets, sidewalks, water, wastewater, power sources, telecommunications, and other facility needs. A community must have the capacity to meet existing needs and plans to meet future expansion and growth needs, as well.

Columbus, Nebraska's economy boasts a greater than average share of manufacturing employment when compared to other Nebraska micropolitan and metropolitan areas. This distinction means that Columbus must constantly maintain and upgrade its public infrastructure. It also works closely with two major railroads and one short-line railroad to provide service to its industries. Columbus recently completed a $6.5 million expansion of its municipal sanitary sewer and storm water system to meet current and future needs. The community works with utility providers to offer first-class services, including telecommunications infrastructure that is so vital to today's industry and local residents.

Kearney, Neb., is another community whose planned growth is necessitating good infrastructure capacity. Kearney's economic development efforts are diversified with emphasis on information technology, transportation, housing development, innovative business retention and recruitment strategies, and infrastructure development. Infrastructure is so important to them that they proudly list the infrastructure development in their community profile. The community is a center for technology infrastructure and highlights digital switching, fiber optics, SONET ring, DSL, wireless and complete business network telecommunications services. Truly, Kearney understands that infrastructure is more than streets and sidewalks.

TECHNOLOGY

Technology development is a niche form of infrastructure development that can offer communities a new beginning. Silicon Valley in California is probably the most famous example of technology development and how it impacted the growth of an area.

In Nebraska, an excellent example of technology development is found in **South Sioux City**. According to its city administrator, South Sioux City was once known for its "used cars and bars". South Sioux City now has many feathers in its cap, including a joint purchasing agreement that allows the city, county, and school district to combine needs and make bulk purchases. Thanks to City Administrator, Lance Hedquist, a technology-oriented spark plug, the city is now recognized as one of the nation's leaders in the use of technology as a development strategy. The city proudly states that it is the "most wired and wireless" city in the United States. It also is the only city in the United States funded as a demonstration project for the U.S. Department of Homeland Security. A tour of its technology capabilities is truly amazing. Schools are protected by a wireless video camera system monitored by the police. A demonstration shows visitors how quickly an intruder can be identified and apprehended within the school. Banks also are included in this protective system.

Additionally, the city council was the first in Nebraska to go "paperless" with city council members depending on emails and website information. Understanding the lifestyle choices of technology–oriented citizens, South Sioux City has invested in a new soccer complex, eight miles of biking and hiking trails, extensive additions to the school, and a new library complete with an aviary and gourmet coffee shop.

Visiting this community, you quickly learn how well they have been able to balance technology investments with quality of life issues. As a matter of fact, "Quality of Life" is the cardinal rule and their adopted mascot – the North American cardinal, is proudly displayed on all official communications, promotional items, and around the community

YOUTH

Ah, youth. Too bad it is wasted on the young (George Bernard Shaw)

Youth is not really wasted, as youth are the future. Helping develop capacity in your local youth will benefit your community now and whichever community they may live in later. Of course, ideally they would return to your community at some point bringing with them all of their skills and ideas. In the meantime, there are several ways to help develop youth capacity and incorporate them into your community and economic development plans.

The Nebraska Community Improvement Program (NCIP), a statewide program that fosters leadership development and recognizes community efforts features a category for Youth Leadership for Outstanding Community Service Awards. There also are many examples of youth who independently see a need in their community and fill that need through their own efforts or in combination with others through formal programs such as 4-H, scouting, church youth groups, or other local organizations.

Ravenna, Neb., had a group of students who saw a need in their community and with encouragement and mentoring found a unique way to make their dream a reality. The youth applied for funding through a Teen Tobacco Prevention program. They were awarded $100,000 to help fund a youth activity center and to educate peers about the danger of tobacco use. Their facility, which is next to the school, provides youth with easy access and a safe place for after school meetings or after game activities. Additionally, the students donated blood and encouraged others to donate blood, helped raise funds for a new Alzheimer's wing at the local nursing home, and wrote and received a $5,000 grant to help support the wing.

In **Sutton, Neb**., the local Future Farmers of America chapter rose to the challenge in developing entrepreneurial-minded youth who often win national recognition for their projects. The chapter has been involved in many local projects including remodeling a home, installing playground equipment, planting trees, installing a fence at a softball field, and constructing a new announcer booth at the baseball field. The students also regularly meet with the chamber and community service committee to discuss upcoming projects. Local FFA Advisor, Thomas Hofmann, "believes it is important for students to learn to value and improve their community during their teen years" according to information shared by the National FFA Organization.

Youth are the future and need to have the opportunity to participate now. Australian Peter Kenyon, founder of I.D.E.A.S. (Initiatives for the Development of Enterprising Action and Strategies), says "*youth are not just the leaders of the future*", as we so often state. Youth should be given the opportunity to be leaders right now as it builds their leadership capacity and also builds additional developmental capacity in the community. Youth bring a variety of skills, talents, and dreams to the challenges. We need to encourage them as we strive to build our developmental capacity.

AND THEY LIVED HAPPILY EVER AFTER
(maybe)

Unfortunately, life is not a fairy tale, a Disney movie, or even a commercial where everyone lives in a "Perfect World". In the real world, dissension happens. Controversy is considered normal in growing and thriving communities. Remember our earlier discussion about storming and norming? One critical element of capacity building is introducing new human capacity opportunities. Yet, every time you add a new member to a group, you need to re-establish the organizational boundaries, figure out the group skill sets, and encourage new relationships. This is not always easy but is an essential part of organizational and human capacity development.

It also is important to discourage "group think" which occurs when groups are pressured to make decisions and members are reluctant to speak out against prevailing suggestions. A Leadership Tips of the Month from www.leadingtoday.org warns us to "*Beware of Groupthink*" describing it as "*the tendency of decision makers to join together around a policy or person without questioning basic assumptions.*" So the member who respectfully plays the Devil's Advocate, raises the questions, or suggests time to reflect may actually be helping to build and maintain followership, leadership, and organizational capacity.

In the *Leadership Secrets of Attila the Hun* (1987), Wess Roberts reminds us, "*Disagreement is not necessarily disloyalty*." (p. 17). Building capacity may not be glamorous or provide a quick answer to your community or organizational needs, but it ultimately offers the proven path to successful long-term development.

The goal of this book has been to help volunteers and community leaders realize some of the dynamics in organizational and community development. The "Tried and True" chapter included case studies of communities that have reached goals by building capacity. The " Doses of Development" chapter is a list of ideas that may jump-start your development efforts by suggesting simple, doable community projects that are not time or finance intensive. Starting with small successes is one way to motivate the community to try larger projects.

My experience working closely with community and economic development issues for more than 25 years has reinforced my belief that capacity building is not only important, it is essential. Communities or organizations that are able to build capacity and weather the vagrancies of time may not live in a "Perfect World" or "happily ever after" but they will survive, develop, and thrive.

Development, it's.... **About Building Capacity.**

About the Author

My formal education includes a Bachelor of Arts with an emphasis in Community Development and a minor in Business Administration. I also have a master's degree in Leadership Development and am pursuing a second masters of science in Organizational Management with an emphasis on Entrepreneurship and Economic Development. Additionally, I am a graduate of the Economic Development Institute and have attended a variety of workshops and seminars on development issues.

Possibly more important than the classroom learning, I have spent most of the past 25 years helping organizations and communities learn how to build capacity. Many of the examples in this book are from my home state of Washington and adopted home state of Nebraska. I hope sharing my own passion for capacity building coupled with examples and success stories highlighted in this book will inspire you to continue to seek ways to build capacity in your organization or community.

REFERENCES:

Cook, James; (n.d); *Community Development Theory*;
    University of Missouri - Columbia

Christenson, James & Robinson, Jr., Jerry; (1989) *Community
    Development in Perspective*, Ames, IA; Iowa State
    University Press

Duening, Thomas & Ivancevich, John, (2003), *Managing
    Organizations,* Cincinnati, OH, Atomic Dog Publishing

Eadie, Douglas; (1997); *Changing by Design*; Jossey-Bass
    Nonprofit Sector Series; San Francisco, CA; Jossey-
    Bass

Kotter, John; (1999) *On What Leaders Really Do*; Harvard
    Business Review Book

Littrell, Donald; (n.d.) *The Theory and Practice of
Community
    Development*; University of Missouri-Columbia

Luther, Vicki and Wall, Milan; (1998) *Clues to Rural
    Community Survival*; Lincoln, NE; Heartland Center
    for Leadership Development

Oakley, Ed and Krug, Doug; (1994); *Enlightened Leadership,
    Getting to the Heart of Change*; New York; Fireside

O'Toole, James (1996); *Leading Change, the Argument for
    Values-Based Leadership,* San Francisco, CA; Jossey-
    Bass

Pulver, Glen and Dodson, David; (1992) *Designing Development Strategies in Small Towns*; Washington, DC; The Aspen Institute

Roberts, Wess; (1987) *Leadership Secrets of Attila the Hun*; New York; Warner Books

Shively, Robert (1997) Small Town Economic Development: Principles of Organization, *Economic Development Review,* Fall, 43-46

Shively, Robert;(2004) *Economic Development for Small Communities: A Handbook for Economic Development Practitioners and Community Leaders*, Washington, D.C.; National Center for Small Communities

Wells, Stuart (1998), *Choosing the Future,* Woburn, MA, Butterworth-Heinemann

www.ingramcontent.com/pod-product-compliance
Lightning Source LLC
Chambersburg PA
CBHW020258290526
45784CB00003B/1286